105

TIPS TO WORK SMART

and think different.

Cynthia Howard RN, PhD, LSSBB

www.worksmartclubnetwork.com

Learn to WORK SMART!

Learning to work smart is more than a cliché. In this digital age, with an overload of information and accelerated demands, it is necessary to learn to manage your energy, focus and attention. Managing your energy <u>increases the time you have</u> to *get it done*.

On the next page, read through the 5 gears that make up the work smart mindset. Use these principles to help you stay energized and achieve success.

Capacity
This is your inner battery. Refresh and rejuvenate your energy.

Curiosity
Ask questions. Be willing to learn new ways of thinking and doing.

Clarity
Knowing what is expected is motivating. Be clear & concise.

Agility
Learn to be flexible and adapt.

Purpose
Knowing what you are doing and why is purpose.

In this booklet, we provide tips that help you rethink how you approach your day. Read one tip each day. Put it into practice.

Too often, when you are caught up in the busyness, or drama, of the day, you lose sight of what is important and what your goals are. The entire day can get lost in busywork. When this is a habit, days turn into weeks and even years, and you miss out on accomplishing your goals.

Stress and pressure make the problem seem bigger than you are. Reframing how you think can break through the feelings of chaos. Apply these simple tips, reframe your thinking, one day at a time.

Many of the tips refer to a course in the Work Smart Club. For membership information, visit **worksmartclubnetwork.com**.

The Work Smart Club is our online Center for Work and Well-being and provides resources to help you advance your career, develop your leadership, manage stress, build resilience, solve problems, and accomplish more than you thought possible.

These resources are available 24/7 and consumable on-the-go in 15 minutes or less. Join the club and turn your device into a learning hub!

To Work SMART, you must THINK DIFFERENTLY.

OVERWHELMED

ANGRY

JOYFUL

SAD

FRUSTRATED

Emotional Checkpoint

DESPAIR

Emotions are like the warning lights on your car's dashboard. They let you know when you need to make a service call.

HAPPY

SCARED

Check in and take action. Ignoring emotions only makes them more intense.

BURNED OUT

SURPRISED

Angry: Set boundaries.
Bored: Step out of your comfort zone.
Disappointed: Reframe your goals
Sad: Let it go.

BETRAYED

EXHAUSTED

ASHAMED

GRATEFUL

SILLY

HURT

BORED

SUSPICIOUS

1.

Breathe Deliberately.

Inhale on a count of 4.

Hold on a count of 4.

Exhale on a count of 4.

Wait 4 seconds before your next breath.

Repeat 4 times.

This is the best way to shift your attention and interrupt the stress reaction.

2.

Water is a natural energizer.

Are you fueling your body or being stimulated by caffeine?

Drink more water.

Drink 24 ounces in the morning before your coffee.

Drink 8 ounces before each meal.

3.

Express gratitude.

This supports the higher functions of your brain – your executive function – keeping your perspective wide and your heart open.

Tell 3 people you appreciate them, today.

4.

Do an inventory of all your projects. Next to each one jot down the number of hours to get this done.

Are you overspending on time?

Are you focusing on the most important projects/ tasks?

5.

Keep a Journal.

When you spend a few moments and think about an experience and write out your thoughts, you are learning and building on your experiences. Reflection helps you grow and develop.

6.

No Whining!

If there is a problem, find a solution.

Stop blaming people, places, or situations.

7.

The power is in the present moment. The present moment is 3 seconds. You can learn a lot when you tune into this moment.

Breathe. Observe. Be present to the moment.

8.

Be nice, no matter what.

When irritated or annoyed, angry, or upset, breathe slowly and deeply, unhook from those raw emotions. Tune into your feelings and deal with them. Do this before you go after that person that triggered your feelings.

9.

Gossip says more about you than the person you are talking about.

If you cannot say something nice, say nothing. Leave every conversation (and situation) better than when you started.

10.

Eat more vegetables.

Vegetables are filled with
minerals.

Minerals are like spark plugs;
they give your body fuel for
sustainable energy.

11.

Show up every day, ready to do your best. This takes planning.

Commit to planning one day a week to focus your activity and intentions for each week. Some people like to do this on a Friday and some on a Sunday.

What day works best for you?

12.

Do a daily review. 5 minutes at the end of every day.

Answer 3 questions:

What worked?

What didn't?

What is next?

13.

Unplug and detox from your devices. Set up technology free zones at work and at home.

Learn to be without your phone.

Relate directly to people around you.

Designate time, every day, when you will unplug; set this time in 1, 2, 3, 4-hour increments.

It takes 5 days for the withdrawal symptoms and fear of missing out (FOMO) to subside. You end up feeling more at peace and relaxed!

14.

Sleep 8 hours (or more).

Your body restores itself at night.

Cutting out sleep is not where you save time.

15.

Pray. Give thanks.

In prayer, ask for the answers to tough questions. Trying too hard to figure everything out gets in the way of making progress.

16.

Holding a grudge is like taking poison and hoping someone else will die. Forgive and move on.

Make a list of people or situations you harbor resentment over. Pick one and write them a letter, that you do not send, and let them know you are ready to move on.

Then shred the letter. Release the anger.

17.

20-minute Rule: Spend 20
minutes of uninterrupted time
every day. Read. Turn off all
distractions.

Be sure you will not be
interrupted.

This exercise builds your
concentration and focus.

18.

Tell jokes. Laugh. Be silly.

You instinctively knew this as a child; play is a great stress reliever.

19.

Therapeutic grade essential oils support your immune system; transform the stress reaction and refresh your senses.

Use essential oils to focus, relax, and shift your mood. Grab your favorite oil and practice deep breathing, inhaling the aroma right from the bottle.

20.

Use F.O.C.U.S. as a problem-solving approach to avoid jumping to solutions.

1. **F**ind the problem. Talk with people closest to it.
2. **O**rganize the information.
3. **C**larify what you know. Ask questions.
4. **U**nderstand the information. Do you need more data?
5. **S**olution. Now you are ready to drill down and find the right solution.

21.

Practice active listening.

Listen ❖ Silent.

Same letters arranged differently.

Lean in. Clear your mind when someone is talking. Listen to what they are saying and ask questions to clarify if you do not understand.

22.

The best revenge is to do what they say you cannot do.

Do not fight resistance or try to prove anything. It drains your energy that is better used going after your goals.

Are you having conversations with people in your head? Turn it off and talk to yourself with positive and inspiring self-talk.

You got this!

23.

Are you focused on what is important (vs urgent)?

Make a list of all your activities, categorize them into 4 categories of the Priority Matrix*:

Important, Urgent.
Important, Not Urgent.
Urgent, Not Important.
Not Important, Not Urgent.

*This is in the Productivity Toolkit, learn about the categories and rethink what you spend your time doing.

24.

Go to bed at a regular time every night.

Put a few drops of lavender essential oil (EO) on a cotton ball to place in your pillowcase.

Sweet dreams.

25.

Use a timer when you are on Social Media.

Schedule your time and take charge of your day.

Staying too long online drains your energy and flattens your focus.

26.

A 15 second distraction
takes 25 minutes to recover
your concentration. Silence
your notifications
on your phone.

Keep your focus.

*Keep an Interruption Log. Find it
online at Work Smart Club.*

27.

Be present to the person you are talking with, make eye contact, nod your head.

Practice active listening.

Being heard is an important basic need. When you lean in and listen, you make people feel special.

28.

Keep a Success journal. Write down your successes, big and small. Then when in doubt read your entries and remember those times when you did it!

29.

Periodically, bathe your senses in
beautiful classical music.

It is calming.

30.

Keep your focus on your goal regardless of how loud, big, or disturbing your distractions are.

Post your goal, written in measurable terms where you can see this every day. This is for personal and work-related goals.

Check out the Goals Toolkit; it is a game changer when it comes to setting goals that stick.

31.

Ask for help.

By asking for help, you are
more approachable in the eyes
of those around you – your team
and your subordinates.

When you ask for help and
listen, you will learn how other
people think and process
information.

32.

Be the CFO of your life: Chief Future Officer.

Write your goals down. Use the reverse planning approach to set milestones.

Take 30 minutes and write out your plan.

33.

Did you know over half the time people are redoing something due to distractions?

Keep an Interruption Log for 2 weeks and look for patterns.

Are you distracting yourself?

34.

When you are hungry, before you reach for the food, ask yourself, "Am I bored, tired, lonely, sad or thirsty?"

Tune into your emotions.

35.

Do you know what your company's mission and vision are? Ever wonder how you contribute to it?

Write out the mission statement and think about how your specific contributions support this statement.

36.

Take a short break every 90 minutes. Stand up, stretch, sip water, run in place, dance. Take 2 minutes to do something physical.

Set your phone timer.

Do not scroll through the internet. This weakens your focus.

This is a power break that will boost your productivity.

37.

You Rock!

It feels good to be appreciated and recognized. Tell your teammate what you like best about working with them.

Write out 2 qualities they bring to the team and share it with them. You can use a note card or tell them in person.

38.

Do you believe in yourself –
without question? Get to know
your strengths and own them.

Write out your top 3 strengths:

1.

2.

3.

What do you do that no one else
does?

39.

Need to improve your speaking skills? Want to learn to think on your feet?

Join Toastmasters, it is a fantastic way to sharpen your presence and be around optimistic people.

40.

Understand the problem before you jump to solutions. Take the time to define the real problem.

Ask questions. Define your desired outcome. Consider alternatives. Before you start fixing, think about the impact each alternative will have on the big picture. Are you fixing one area only to create issues elsewhere?

41.

Focus and finish what you start.

Set up a plan to finish your projects that are incomplete. Check out Tip #4. On the inventory of your projects, which ones are undone?

Did you know unfinished projects take up internal bandwidth, wasting energy and limiting your thinking power available for other projects and ideas?

42.

Foundational habits like sleep, diet, exercise and even money management, set the tone for developing habits for high performance.

Use the Habit Tracker, available in the Work Smart Club, to track your habits for 2 weeks.

Are you consistent?

43.

Don't complain. Don't explain.

This weakens your confidence. Are you trying to please people with an explanation? Get permission?

44.

What motivates you to do great work?

Money?
Creativity?
Recognition?
Approval?

Think about what motivates you in this situation; provide more of that motivation.

45.

Do you know what your priority is for today?

Do your activities line up with this priority?

Micro-habits for success:

1. Write your goals and priorities down.

2. Read through them frequently.

3. Simplify your daily 'to-do' list.

46.

Optimists' see things as temporary. They are known to say, *"There is nothing as constant as change."*

Be positive.

Pessimists see things as permanent, pervasive, and personal. They are known to say, *"Nothing good ever happens to me!"*

47.

Use the mood chart, on page 8, and identify your feelings. Check in 1-2x a day.

Researchers have found that emotions that you can name, you can tame. Expand your feelings vocabulary.

48.

It makes me angry when...

Make a list of all the situations, things and people that make you angry. Keep track of your triggers and change your reaction.

49.

My ideal day looks like...

Describe your day.
Now replicate it.

50.

Did you know that hard work is inspiring? Working hard is not what drains your energy. It is the depleting emotions throughout the day that drain your energy and get you off track.

Track how often you are impatient, annoyed, or irritable. This is costing you energy and focus.

Plug your energy leaks.

51.

Think of a time recently when you overreacted. As you think about it, practice gratitude breathing and release the tension, forgive yourself, and let it go.

After 30 seconds to 1 minute of breathing, how could you have done it differently?

Gratitude breathing is inhaling the feeling of gratitude deeply and slowly and exhaling frustration deeply and slowly. Repeat.

52.

Your health is your greatest asset.
Not money or time. Are you
making lifestyle choices that
support vibrant health?

53.

Are you focused on what is ahead of you or what happened last week, month, year?

If you are often tired, sluggish, or feeling blah, you are focused on problems, rather than looking at solutions.

54.

Cut down on coffee. Drink water instead. It is a natural energizer and flushes out toxins.

Exchange your "first thing" in the morning coffee with 12 ounces of water.

55.

MOVE MORE.

Walk, dance, run, bounce, hip hop – move your body, 15 minutes a day.

This boosts your productivity by 15%.

56.

Detox from drama. Refuse to give in to gossip, drama, ongoing sagas that other people bring you.

Resist gossip. Leave the conversation better than when you started.

57.

Appreciate your boss. Send a "Thank You" note to your Boss for something you appreciate. Bosses are people too!

58.

Just for today adopt an optimistic attitude.

Optimists' are realistic – they see the challenges and they believe in their ability to handle it. They resist overthinking and going through disaster scenarios.

59.

Your emotions are what energize you – or not. If you are avoiding feeling angry, you are also shutting down your ability to be happy.

Are you shutting down your flow?

Deal with your emotions, stop avoiding them.

60.

What is your favorite color?
Wear it more often.

61.

Being self-aware helps you understand yourself.

It also helps you tune into others. Take the time to figure out what you are feeling and why.

62.

Visualization can turn negative energy into positive. Worry is the default use of visualization.

Be intentional with your thoughts. What do you *want to have happen?*

Focus on that rather than what already happened or what might happen.

63.

Every 90 minutes your body and mind go through a natural cycle and attention decreases.

Every 90 minutes to 2 hours, deep breathe, sip water, stretch.

64.

When given feedback, open your mind, close your mouth, and listen. Say thank you and evaluate it later. Avoid being defensive.

65.

Burnout is a slippery slope of isolating, not caring and shutting down.

Are you on that slope?

Ask for help.

[The Work Smart Club is filled with resources. Keep in mind, you also need to connect with humans!]

66.

Over-care is not a sign of being more caring – it is caring too much. If you feel like you are "strong enough" for everyone, or you worry, you might over-care.

Empathy is recognizing and acknowledging the other person. It is not taking on their burdens. Set boundaries over what is yours and what is someone else's burden.

67.

Resilience is your capacity. It is grit, courage, optimism, forward, future focus, persistence.

It is the ability to embrace the challenge. Sometimes, it just requires you to stick it out.

Hang in there. Do not quit.

68.

Strategic thinking knows what box to think outside of – are you clear about your main objective?

What is the most important job to be done?

69.

The constant flow of distraction
makes it harder to remember
details. Make a habit of writing
things down.

70.

Emotional intelligence (Ei) is your ability to relate to others – this means you know what is going on, *in you,* and give them your full attention.

Do you know how you come across to others?

71.

Everyday Ei is as simple as smiling at someone and making eye contact. Let that person know you see them and acknowledge them.

72.

Stretch your comfort zone.
Take a risk that moves you
closer to your goals.

What is your stretch goal?

73.

Keep your running shoes next to your bed. As soon as you wake up, put them on and go for that walk or run.

74.

Are you clear on what is expected of you at work?

Download the Job Analysis in the Work Smart Club. Work through it, and then meet with your Boss. Get feedback from them on their priority.

75.

Breathe. Smile.

Drink water.

Move.

Repeat often.

76.

Set up an email policy and review mail at set times during the day.

Practice the 2-minute rule: if you can respond in 2 minutes then do it, otherwise file it for the scheduled time to handle mail.

77.

Double sevens is a lucky number!

Success is not about luck.

Is your confidence built on a belief in you, or that your success was due to a lucky break, someone you knew or how you look?

Get out of the Imposter Syndrome and own your strengths.

78.

Establish a new habit of exercising your core. Do 10 minutes of crunches, sit ups, the plank - every morning and evening.

Strengthen your core and energize your body.

79.

Fighting off worry? Your boss, jealous coworker, negative nellie at work, disrespectful teen, aging parents...

The list can be long. Worry doesn't change anything and will make it harder to see opportunities. Make a list of all the worries and fears, getting them out of your head and on paper immediately decreases their power.

80.

Water decreases appetite and naturally energizes you. Drinking more water is the single most important thing you can do to increase your energy.

Drink water instead of coffee or soda.

81.

Status Quo: Continuing to do what you have always done – *even when it is not working*. What do you need to do, differently, to get the results you want?

82.

Do you talk about problems or solutions? When you lead with solutions and ideas, people are naturally attracted to you.

83.

Practice the Attention Reboot.

Imagine you are seeing everything
for the first time – as if you have
never experienced it before.

84.

It is natural for your mind to wander. Practice bringing yourself into the present moment. Let other thoughts drift away.

Being mindful increases your satisfaction and happiness.

85.

What are 3 things you do now,
every day, that help you achieve
your goals:

1.

2.

3.

Do more of what is working!

86.

Distraction increases irritability.
Do one thing at a time. You will
get more done and enjoy your day.

What is your typical multi-task?
Eating while reading, scrolling on
computer, talking on phone?

Make a point to just do one thing.
Notice how it was different? What
happened to your energy level?

87.

Do you feel stuck? Going over and over the situation in your mind and getting nowhere?

Breathe in peace and gratitude on a count of 4. Hold your breath on a count of 4. Exhale frustration on a count of 4. Wait 4 seconds before your next breath. Repeat.

Now look at the situation.

What's changed?

88.

What is the number 1 priority for you today?

Are you on track?

89.

Express your BEST self – no matter what.

What gets in the way of you showing up at your best? Do you tell yourself the following?

I am tired, don't feel like it, or what difference does it make?

What can you do to change that?

90.

Enjoy more face-to-face time with people you know. Call someone, walk over to their office. Get out from behind technology.

91.

What is important is seldom
urgent and what is urgent is
seldom important.

Are you stuck putting out fires?
Prioritize.

92.

Spread good news.

Celebrate other people's achievements.

93.

Manage your energy and you have all the time you need. It all boils down to what you eat, what you drink and what you think.

Keep a log of what you eat and drink. Also track your thoughts.

Any patterns?

94.

Being busy is not the same as being productive. How do you know you are focused on what is most important?

Do you have measurable goals?

95.

How is work? What do you need to do to excel at your job?

Skills needed:

Attitude:

96.

When you are at work, be at work.

When you are at home, be at home.

Be 100% available to what you are doing and who you are with.

97.

What is your 2-year plan for your career?

Do a reverse plan.

1. Establish where you want to be in 2 years.

2. Write down all the steps to get there.

3. Break it into monthly goals.

98.

50% of time spent is recovering from interruptions.

Ever wondered how much time is wasted? Calculate it:

Number of times you are interrupted per hour:

Amount of time it takes to get back to what you were doing:

99.

Use 1 drop of peppermint essential oil in a quart of water or a quart of tea. Refresh yourself. Get focused.

100.

Do you compulsively check your phone? Put it away during parts of the day. Check it at scheduled intervals.

101.

Practice the Wonder Woman
stance. Feet shoulder width apart,
hands on hips. Head up. Breathe
in and out and feel the connection
under your feet. Let the tension
flow out.

102.

Your ability to focus will determine your success.

Eliminate distractions and interruptions.

103.

Write out your goals.

Write out your plan for the day.

Writing helps you clarify what is important and increases your commitment to achieve that goal.

Keep this goal where you can see it every day. This engages your right brain, operating subconsciously, and will guide you to achieve this goal.

104.

Think the best about people and about outcomes. What most people worry about, never happens. See the best in your coworkers. Think the best about situations.

Believe the best about yourself.

105.

Break things into small manageable tasks. Put them on your calendar in a timeline. Every day accomplish these mini tasks, keeping the end result in mind.

NOTES

www.ingramcontent.com/pod-product-compliance
Lightning Source LLC
Chambersburg PA
CBHW061608220326
41598CB00024BC/3497